LAUGHING MATTERS

RIDDLES

DUNCE

Detention

Compiled by Pam Rosenberg   Illustrated by Patrick Girouard

Special thanks to Katie Cottrell for her assistance in compiling source materials.

Published in the United States of America by The Child's World®
P.O. Box 326, Chanhassen, MN 55317-0326
800-599-READ
www.childsworld.com

Acknowledgments
The Child's World®: Mary Berendes, Publishing Director

Editorial Directions, Inc.: E. Russell Primm, Editorial Director and Line Editor; Katie Marsico, Assistant Editor; Matthew Messbarger, Editorial Assistant; Susan Hindman and Susan Ashley, Proofreaders

The Design Lab: Kathleen Petelinsek, Designer and Page Production

Registration

Library of Congress Cataloging-in-Publication Data
Rosenberg, Pam.
  Riddles / compiled by Pam Rosenberg ; illustrated by Patrick Girouard.
    p. cm. — (Laughing matters)
Summary: Simple riddles on a variety of subjects.
  ISBN 1-59296-076-6 (alk. paper)
  1. Riddles, Juvenile. [1. Riddles.] I. Girouard, Patrick, ill. II. Title.
III. Series.
  PN6371.5.R58   2004
  818'.602—dc28   2003018086

WHAT?

What does an invisible cat drink? Evaporated milk.

flower

What's smarter than a talking parrot? A spelling bee.

What kind of dog always knows the time? A watchdog.

What do you call a cat in the desert? Sandy Claws.

What do snakes do after they have an argument?
  They hiss and make up.

What's an elephant's favorite way to travel?
  By jumbo jet.

What's a cheetah's favorite food?
  Fast food.

What's gray, has big ears, and a trunk?
  A mouse going on vacation.

What time is it when an elephant sits in your car?
  Time to get a new car.

What do frogs like to eat with their hamburgers?
  French flies.

What shoes do frogs wear?
  Open-toad sandals.

What did the teddy bear say when asked if she
wanted lunch?
  No thanks, I'm stuffed.

4

What begins with an E and ends with an E but only has one letter in it?
An envelope.

What starts with a P, ends with an E, and has thousands of letters in it?
The post office.

What's always at the end of a rainbow?
The letter W.

What word has ten letters and starts with G-A-S?
Automobile.

What goes all around the yard but never moves?
A fence.

What has 88 keys but not a single door?
A piano.

5

What runs up and down the stairs but never moves at all?
The carpet.

What kind of building always has the most stories?
A library.

What is black and white, black and white, black and white?
A penguin rolling down a hill.

What do gingerbread boys put on their beds?
Cookie sheets.

What did the zero say to the eight?
Nice belt.

What has wheels and flies?
A garbage truck.

What kind of barbecue grill does a spider use? A Web-er.

7

What kind of pants do flowers wear?
    Petal pushers.

What is faster, heat or cold?
    Heat. You can catch a cold.

What comes up when the rain goes down?
    An umbrella.

What did one math book say to the other math book?
    Have I got problems!

What is the laziest mountain in the world?
    Mount Ever-rest.

What did the sea say to the shore?
    Nothing, it just waved.

What did the envelope say to the stamp?
    Stick with me and we'll go places.

What state is on a horse?
    Maine.

What state is high in the middle and round at both ends?
Ohio.

What travels all around the world but stays in one corner?
A postage stamp.

What state wears glasses?
Mississippi. It has four I's.

What did Cinderella say when her pictures weren't in at the photo shop?
Some-day my prints will come!

What state is inside another state?
Kansas is inside Arkansas.

What clothes did Delaware?
A New Jersey.

What's the difference between a coyote and a flea?
One howls on the prairie and the other one prowls on the hairy.

What's the penguin's favorite aunt?
Aunt-Arctica.

What is a puppy after it is five days old?
Six days old.

What should you do if your puppy chews on your dictionary?
Take the words right out of his mouth.

What's another word for a mousetrap?
Cat.

WHAT DO YOU GET?

What do you get when you cross a centipede with a parrot? A walkie-talkie.

11

What do you get when you cross a tiger with a canary? I don't know, but when it sings, you'd better listen!

What do you get when you cross a piranha with a flower? I don't know, but I wouldn't try to smell it if I were you!

What do you get when you cross a centipede with a chicken? Enough drumsticks for an army.

What do you get when you cross a skunk with an angel? Something that stinks to high heaven.

What do you get when you cross a sheet with a porcupine? An animal that knits its own sweaters.

What do you get when you walk through a field of four-leaf clovers and poison ivy?

A rash of good luck.

What happened to the man who crossed an electric blanket with a toaster?

He kept popping out of bed all night.

What do you get when you cross a kangaroo and a snake?

A jump rope!

What do you get when you cross a mosquito with a computer?

A lot of bytes.

What do you get when you put corn holders into sweet corn?

Pierced ears.

What do you get when you cross a man in a new suit with a crocodile?

A snappy dresser.

What do you
call a rabbit
with fleas?
   Bugs Bunny.

WHAT DO YOU CALL?

What do you call a boy
who's always lying on the floor?
   Matt.

What do you call a boy with a seagull on his head?
   Cliff.

What do you call a girl who always carries an
encyclopedia in her pocket?
   Smarty pants.

What do you call it when a lamb sneaks up on
someone?
   A lambush.

What do you call Frosty the Snowman in July?
   A puddle.

14

WHY?

Why do hummingbirds hum? Because they don't know the words.

Why did the gingerbread boy stay home from school? He felt crummy.

Why do bees have sticky hair? Because they use a honeycomb.

Why is it a good idea to plant bulbs in your garden? So the worms can see where they are going.

Why are flowers so lazy? Because you always find them in beds.

Why did the silly kid throw butter out the window? He wanted to see a butterfly.

Why was the baby ant so confused? Because all of her uncles were ants.

15

Why were the baby strawberries crying?
Because their parents were in a jam.

Why did the duck get detention at school?
Because he was always making wise quacks.

Why isn't a bank a good place to keep a secret?
Because it's filled with tellers.

Why did the girls wear bathing suits to school?
They rode in a car-pool.

Why shouldn't you tell a secret to a pig?
Because he's a squealer.

Why did the silly kid throw a glass of water out the window?
He wanted to see a waterfall.

Why did the firefly get bad grades in school?
It wasn't very bright.

Why is it hard for a ladybug to hide?
Because she's always spotted.

Why did the dance teacher give up tap dancing?
She kept falling in the sink.

Why does a ballerina wear a tutu?
Because the one-one's too small and the
three-three's too big.

Why is Florida the funniest state in the nation?
Because it's a pun-insula.

Why would a heart be a good musical instrument?
It has a great beat.

Why did the teacher turn the classroom lights on?
Because her students were so dim.

Why was Snow White chosen to be a judge?
Because everyone said she was the
fairest one of all.

Why did the chicken cross the road?
To get to the other side.

Why did the rooster cross the road?
To prove he wasn't a chicken.

Why did the bubblegum cross the road?
It was stuck to the chicken's leg.

Why did the frog cross the road?
To see what the chicken was doing.

Why did the farmer cross the road?
To catch all the chickens.

Why didn't the skeleton cross the road?
It didn't have the guts.

HOW MANY?

How many animals did Moses take on the ark? None. It was Noah.

How many feet are in a yard? That depends on how many people are standing in it.

How many letters are in the alphabet? Eleven.

How many sheep does it take to knit a sweater? None. They can't knit.

21

WHERE?

Where does a sheep get a haircut?
At the baabaa shop.

Where does success come before work?
In the dictionary.

Where is the best place to hide a chocolate?
In your mouth.

Where do cows go for their vacation?
Moo York.

IF?

If you drop a yellow hat in the Red Sea, what does it become? Wet.

If you have nine oranges in one hand and eight in the other, what do you have? Big hands!

If athletes get athlete's foot, what do astronauts get? Mistle-toe.

If Mississippi gave Missouri her New Jersey, what would Delaware? I don't know, Alaska.

About Patrick Girouard:

Patrick Girouard has been illustrating books for almost 15 years but still looks remarkably lifelike. He loves reading, movies, coffee, robots, a beautiful red-haired lady named Rita, and especially his sons, Marc and Max. Here's an interesting fact: A dog named Sam lives under his drawing board. You can visit him (Patrick, not Sam) at www.pgirouard.com.

About Pam Rosenberg:

Pam Rosenberg is a former junior high school teacher and corporate trainer. She currently works as an author, editor, and the mother of Sarah and Jake. She took on this project as a service to all her fellow parents of young children. At least now their kids will have lots of jokes to choose from when looking for the one they will tell their parents over and over and over again!